Toss Me to the Waiting Sky

Mary M Carlisle

Mary Margaret Carlisle

Poetry
in the
Arts

www.poetryinarts.org

SECOND EDITION

Copyright © 2009 Mary Margaret Carlisle

Cover Photo — Mary Margaret Carlisle

Published in the United States of America
Poetry in the Arts, Inc.
http://www.poetryinarts.org
All Rights Reserved

ISBN 978-0-9840843-1-9

Printed by Instantpublisher.com

Foreword

A longtime and distinguished editor and teacher, Mary Margaret Carlisle has also been a tireless promoter not only of the art of poetry but also of legions of its practitioners, both "budding" and experienced. She founded the Gulf Coast Poets chapter of the Poetry Society of Texas, and her name has become synonymous with "poetry" in the Webster/Clear Lake/Galveston area of the Lone Star State. It should come as no surprise, therefore, that her first and long past due book-length collection of poetry, *Toss Me to the Waiting Sky*, is an impressive poetic achievement, in range of subject matter, poetic craft, and raw emotional honesty. Although she writes most memorably about family and the glories of the natural world, Carlisle's subjects also include vanilla tofutti, the Columbia shuttle disaster, the Obama inauguration, a painting by Edouard Manet, and hurricane refugees.

Her poems about her father and children are especially poignant. She writes of her father "...dressing early / in dark aching cold and creeping / down to the weary furnace"; and of him "...slowing with the seasons / coming at last to a natural end." She writes of her daughter as "the bread I made / with the heat of my heart..." And she writes of her son doing his laundry for the first time; about how she misses him "and his pockets / heavy with expectation / and the joy of being free."

When Carlisle turns her poetic eye to the natural world, she captures it with powerful immediacy and strikingly original imagery. Her coracle moon "travels its boatly way / past the mountain peaks / of across-the-way / houses and garages..."; her dawn sky's "...a dented sheet of aluminum / or even a beaten-pewter racing-Ferrari..."; and her raven's caws "...cling / to dark shadows..." In "Tethered in Llano Estacado," Carlisle frees a mallard from a tether tangled around his legs, and uses his return to the sky as a metaphor for her own fate: "I wonder – will I fly off alone / when life's sharp knife cuts me free? / Or will I wait for someone else / to toss me to the waiting sky?" The poet was so powerfully moved by the event, whether actual or imaginary, that she titled the collection with a portion of the poem's last line.

Carlisle's keen sense of poetic craft is evident in her skillfully executed ekphrastic poem, "Branch of White Peonies and Pruning Shears." Employing short, compressed lines with carefully selected modifiers, the poet captures the visual essence of Manet's painting while going well beyond the constraints of mere description. The painter's roses, "newly shorn / by a barely revealed / pair of pruning shears..." become "...memories / of our mother's gardens / folded next to our hearts..." Her short lines are musical with assonance and alliteration, reaching a haunting crescendo at the poem's end: "...peonies rest / their crumpled shrouds / incarnate within / Manet's intent."

Larry D. Thomas, 2008-2009 Texas State Poet Laureate

Contents

Contents

Remembered in Rose

I like the spring fields
where horses wander without halters
rough coats shedding hanks.

Summer edges down ploughed furrows
where grasses grow in waves
green stems tipped with shimmer

in a leaning river of faded rose
the same color found in the painted gowns
of confederate ladies.

Those gentlewomen stare sternly from a time
when cotton filled planter's sheds
and black sweat bought homes, gowns, and horses.

The earth itself remembers those days
in crumbling plantations, glistening taffeta grass
and thoroughbreds drifting beside Forty Acres Road.

the immutable law of mowing grass

flow supposedly happens
when mind, body, and spirit
focus during a series of moments flowing
without effort towards the same end
and time stops
like a runner's high
floating you along
each moment sung into being

you can get to that feeling
slicing grass with a hand pushed mower
grass blades and metal blades frozen
as if a breath in winter
and a smell fresh as snow
drifting across the lawn
all is quiet except the whir
of mower
and you —
breathing

Prayer for a Southern Wind

the man across the street
is anchored to his yard
he thinks of low seas and tepid winds
and of his wave runner waiting in the drive
he trims around his girlfriend's amaryllis
soon to bloom as bright a red as his ski boat
Sunday devotions mean kneeling
in the lily bed and pulling spindly weeds
sweeping pecan leaves and pine needles
from an endless horizon of dusty street
his devotions a meditation
on speeding across a quiet Texas bay
into a benediction of sunlight

mockingbird riff

the blue jay's call
rockets out
shrill staccato chops
defining territory
but not as melodic
as the endless cries
of the mockingbird's
in-the-pocket patter
like a finger
flipped at all
interlopers
its backbeat bebop riff
repeated and repeated
from rooftop
oleander
mailbox
in minor scale mode
a turnaround series
sung or trilled
meaningless
cipher to us
but a saucy
love cry
to his mate
that needs
no translation
pure
jazz
bird

In Medias Res

In the poor-dirt Texas lowlands
Grandpa found himself a poor Missionary Baptist Church
that needed itself a Spanish-speaking pastor.
Blake's hands ink-stained from writing
sermons, he taught the love of God
existed not just in church but in the wheat fields
fruit groves, and beyond.

Grandma discovered an abandoned farm orchard
thirty acres planted in three kinds of nuts.
On her knees more than Blake
she crawled on the ground, dragging and filling
a tattered quilt with nuts, emptying them
into old flour sacks then back to crawling on all fours.
She traded boxes and bags of walnuts and pecans
for flour sugar and butter, and baked their church up into
solvency.
As her own children grew, Maudie taught
the neighbor's kids out in the orchard
showing the A B C's of geese migrating
the coolness of stars in cloudless skies
and how to read and write.

Every Christmas Eve, fifty migrant families walked
over to Grandpa Carlisle's church, five miles
in rain or snow through the empty fields
with the ringing of hand bells
in the hands of their children
to praise the birth of the baby Jesus
the kindness of love and honesty.

Between Blake and Maudie they found
there was always room for one more chair or child or family
that truth and love lies between extremes
like the north wind bringing sunshine or snow
and that the last piece of pecan pie should always
be eaten with two forks and laughter.

tincan summer

daddy punched holes in the bottom of an empty corn can
filled it with compost he'd made in a chickenwire bin
out past the back-back-yard behind the garage
he pushed the seed down into that rich black earth
it was just a peach pit in an old tin can
but over the summer we watched and waited
for my gold he said

the cherries had all been picked and the
last of the plums disappeared from the crisping
drawer of the old white Frigidaire
when a tiny shoot appeared unfurling three leaves
dark green shiny leaves, tough leaves of
forest green leather that would fold but not tear

we planted it in the middle-yard,
away from mother's laundry lines and the
long raised bed of her neatly tended hybrid roses

the peach tree grew wide and very tall
but for many years its friendly branches leaned low
where even the smallest child could pick armloads
of daddy's tincan summer gold

dipping crawdads

in the bottom of a pebbled creek
fat crawdads dart under leaves
behind water-smoothed stones
and dive into whirling eddies
but daddy, in long black waders
nets slow and quick alike
and drops each squirmy catch
into a heavy aluminum bucket
held out of her reach
by her laughing brother
she wants to help hold or net
but is told she is too small
next year will come her turn
she cannot see that far ahead
only into the clear fast creek
but even then she is convinced
she will always be too small
too young or not quite ready
her brother — first loved
so much brighter than the rest —
he will always hold the bucket
as everything dips into his hands

Father and the Furnace

Sundays too my father dressed early
in dark aching cold and crept
down to the weary furnace.
With black scorched fire tongs
drew out noxious snakes
of long glowing clinkers
tossed them in a metal barrel
then shoveled coal from the dark bin
onto the embers.
The house shivered and creaked as it warmed;
frost melted away from the windowpanes.
Mother would rouse at last and call us
to a room made warm by my father.

In all the years I lived at home
father never used an alarm clock;
even after they changed to oil heat
he rose early every day ~ perhaps
the memory of the furnace waiting
to blaze at his touch awoke him.
He said once the furnace
was the only thing in our cold house
to ever give back more than it took.

Perennial

I remember Father, hoe in hand
broke earth in spring, patiently
picked out grubs, stones, sticks
smoothed earth to accept
and welcome each small seed

Later we sat on the stoop
ate sandwiches, fresh bread
slathered with mayonnaise
crisp lettuce piled high
with thick, newly picked
tomatoes – a spring of summer thyme

In autumn, back bent with another year's work
Father chopped down withered tomato stalks
sharpened his gardening tools one more time
on the old round hone
and prepared to rest out winter

The longest lasting perennial in his garden
was Father, slowing with the seasons
coming at last to a natural end
thoughts of him fade
into winter's fallow fields
but green again in the spring.

my daughter

you are the bread I made
with the heat of my heart
and the kneading of my hands
sweet bread
made of all things good
baked in the oven of love
placed reverently
on life's table
you are the bread I made
yet you have made me
with your love
you are
the sustenance
of my life

my son

the first time
you did the laundry
three small rocks
a handful of pennies
and a broken stick
rattled around for an hour
in the washing machine
testament to a boyhood
filled with exploration
oh, my boy, how I miss you
and your pockets
heavy with expectation
and the joy of being free

two fortunate

lunch was as always
delicious and plentiful
a chopstick heaven

just one buffet trip
plus a delivery from
we cook your choices

sliced apple dessert
tart-sweet strawberry Jell-O
without the whipped cream

the check arrives with
two packaged fortune cookies
I snatch up the first

he gets two fortunes
mine is totally empty
we both laugh aloud

I have no fortune
perhaps that is for the best
he shares – I accept

Is that Rain on the Roof?

The background of night
is the drone of highway traffic
hum of a neighbor's air conditioner
song of summer cicadas.
Clocks tick louder and more often
and the bathroom faucet drips and drips.
You turn and twist as if you're swimming
in the waters of Galveston Bay
but your arms, hampered by a thin sheet
take no strokes, only your feet kick
and hands twitch. The usual quiet stretch
between light's out and dawn seems
endlessly interrupted by small noises
and the mockingbird atop
our fireplace chimmney
opens and closes the golf umbrella
of sleep so often
silent midnight wakes us all.

In my Native Tongue

on Queen Ann street
rows of rough red brick houses
each touched with gray mortar
six long steps rise
to origami squares of covered porches

in the seventh house from the end
stored in a cool basement converted coal bin
shelves filled with mason jars of strawberry jam
apricot butter, spiced brandied peaches
still await a feather duster

upstairs in a tiny kitchen
wooden chairs scraped groves
in beige linoleum scrubbed so many times
black diamond patterns fade
beneath the bleach

behind the house
two old oaks so strongly grew into each other
one trunk lifted both sets of branches
there, in deep shade, my sister
you and I traded rhythm and cadence
a particular way of speaking without accent
Midwest imprinted on each word

a tongue that still speaks
of my Missouri home

River Road Mantras

Our flat was six floors up
one long room divided by folding walls
tiny bath tucked behind the Murphy bed
kitchen pinched into an alcove
baby's bassinet five steps from the front door.
One wall was nothing but windows
we kept the blinds closed day and night
but not the windows.
We were so close to another complex
we were treated every night to Frank Sinatra
records played across the courtyard.
Our cat was mean as a half/Siamese can be
bit anyone who tried to pet him.
Maybe we had him fixed too soon–
he went from sweet to nasty overnight,
but we had the baby and we both loved him.
You and I weren't really in love
though there were moments when love seemed real enough
like when you moved us back down to Texas
and crooned Frank Sinatra songs like mantras
as we drove the Red River road south
all the way to the Piney Woods

Shearing

You sit not still but without speaking
on the battered backless stool
swinging your feet in unison
to the tuneless song you hum.
Your hunkered young back
turned to me, your head rocking a bit
as I slide clippers over curls
grown for the last two years.
A burr, you demand, so I free your pale scalp
from the weight of heavy hair.
It's to be your last hair cut
until high school graduation,
but we don't know that then
about the hair or the many rebellions
set to bubble beneath the shearing
in your imaginative mind.
You'll join a garage band of guitarists
play loud tunes that rock the house
and shake the neighbors.
You'll create new ways to protest
and will unstring your guitar,
but right now you're kicking your feet
and humming. Buddha smiling
before everything else follows.

Lost Peak Touches Heaven

There is a picture in my mind, you with the sun
rising behind you, a buttermilk sky all pink
and blue with promise. Somewhere out along
Dog Canyon Trail, you think you're crossing
an arroyo to make Manzanita Ridge. You
want to sit on top where the trail levels off
before the path drops steeply down again.

You're searching for Guadalupe, tallest Texas
mountain, its peak wreathed in smoky clouds
but you've made a bad turn. You see alligator
juniper and ponderosa pine, chinkapin oak
and big tooth maple instead of block boulders.

You're lost on the Tejas Trail, about to cross
canyon bottom to scale Lost Peak, where you'll
break both legs, run out of food then water
and time, your last photograph of an eagle flying.

At church they said you were mountain lost
but heaven found. I have your last photos
and see everywhere you've been. I say
I just can't see you dead. I know I'll always
see you climbing.

the coracle moon

travels its boatly way
past the mountain peaks
of across-the-way
houses and garages
faintly golden gleaming
a dream ship
gliding heedless
stars too far
and faint to roughen
its midnight skysea

there is no price
for passage
no sails to lift
to catch a breeze
no decks to scrub
just the slip of moon
coursing steadily by
leaving no wake
behind but sleep

Monotype

It's the kind of sky
at dawn you might have called sad
or perhaps a dented sheet of aluminum
or even a beaten-pewter racing-Ferrari

but by mid-morning it's bright and pearly
like your well-worn Peter Belisi silk scarf.
After rain, it reflects like crystal dew
stippled onto fallen leaves.

By noon it folds Payne's gray into white on blue
then by turns is dun, drab, dingy, leaden
changing from a chiaroscuro Caravaggio
into an enamel Limoges grisaille.

All afternoon, it tones up then down into slate
stone, ash, old silver, mouse gray
until at dusk, above your scraped granite slab
twilight spreads dark and dull.

rosemary for remembrance

for desperate hours   wind splinters glass windows
doors groan crash   the house sways
heavy rain bombs the roof
rolling waves break near the oldest trees
the oak goes down   roots rip straight up
splitting the house in two   doors force open
slam shut slam open a knocking that does not end
curtains whip out and back and out again
wrap broken branches that empty of leaves
pine needles sew themselves into the back of a velvet settee
the roof tears off and up   the wind roars screaming
until a wordless silence drops
into the darkness
the only light a circle of stars until rain returns
followed by wind and it begins again
the seagreen rug becomes the sea
debris scrapes past shattered windows
a baby buggy floats in the backyard sandbox
a cat lies limp in the spinning spokes of a tireless bicycle
the only color gray   gray   gray
until it's finally quiet
but for the drip drip drip of water from the ceiling
and a call from a passing boat gathers
us into the safety of a trembling ride
dankness and darkness overpowering everything
except for a trace of rosemary
where our welcoming gate once stood

Gadwall Duck Pond, West Texas

The bird lifts, slowly at first, feet dragging on the pond
but with powerful wing-beats breaks free
up and up and higher than the trees, yet circles round.
A single drop of water falls into the eclipse
of ripples that mark where he had rested, then he is gone.
The pond quiets. No touch of wind mars the glass
reflection of a chilling empty sky.
No echoes cross the silent shore.
It is early winter. Alone all autumn, he won't be back.

I've not been able to paint, write or even think.
I could chop another cord of logs
to stack beside the door before the flurries fall
or just give up, go home.
It's just so quiet. Can I make it though winter?
Maybe I should close the cabin. Sell it. Buy a single condo
in the city. Get a computer, TV, a telephone.

I reach for the paddle. Transfixed by a cry
beyond the trees, I hesitate, look up. He comes again
this time with another. A mate?
In the twilight of the cloudless sunset
they slice silently, splashlessly onto the pond
swim close to my canoe
call softly back and forth. Settle in.

So do I.

catchfly

breathtaking rose red
your clustered flowers
lift from lush valleys
and rise among dun
mountain rocks and boulders
slender stems
unbroken by storm
you bow before the wind
with the grace
of a nun in prayer
holding fast
a rosary of insects
trapped in sticky sap

Coyote

the Bridge for Prosperity
between El Paso and Cd Juarez
is crowded with tourists
but the water beneath is slow
so you swim the Rio Grande
roll yourself dry in the dusty sand
howl at dawn's traffic-flag orange
and trot off to find something to eat

maybe a pampered lapdog or two
easy to snatch out of a backyard
you can jump six feet easy
neighbors won't complain too loud
if you leave the garbage cans alone

your last meal was carrion
but you'll eat most anything
frogs, snakes, poultry, even fruit
ah, Chihuahua!
now you're hungry for a little Mexican food

A Cautionary Guide to Nature

Lest you wish to over-rhapsodize
about the loveliness of nature
forget-you-not:
even if poisonous snakes, freakish storms
or mountain blizzards pass you gently by
for each majestic canyon bend
and every stunning natural vista
you can still look forward
to the perpetual attendance
of ticks, fleas, flies, mosquitoes
and the also present eagerness
of biting ants and stinging caterpillars —
nature's way of discouraging
those dainty souls who
have previously only viewed from afar
rather than experiencing the natural world
up close and personal.

Bajada

Dust devils swirl up in these lands
yet there is a fine silence here
a stillness between mountain ranges
worn down to grit by wind, water and time.
Creosote marks a climate change
where the desert offers sand and stones,
a buttermilk sky of chrysanthemum,
and tufts of coyote fur caught in the spiny
whips of ocotillo flaming into bloom.

In the alluvial fan of the bajada,
a black-tailed viper coils in scant shade
beneath a fish-hook cactus,
warns, do not pause
rattling tail and sharp-spines
forgive no missteps,
abandon this brooding playa
to the wind.

With the Moon for a Lantern

down a step or two away
the canyon awaits

its steep rocky walls
dusted by a sliver of breeze

raven's caws cling
to dark shadows

deadened echoes
submerge like stars

trapped in deep sediment
of the quiet lake below

Watching Pigeons at the Velero

the stack-up of birds
along the phone lines over the gas station
seems to follow a certain protocol
large pigeons drop down with wings extended
force smaller birds out of the way
who fly to the next line down
and jostle for position between even smaller birds

for a few minutes every morning
the confusion is so great
a pair of red-tailed hawks
waiting atop the telephone pole
take their pick of the fat birds on top
folding wings and diving
aiming not for the biggest or smallest target
but those forced to the ends of the group
upon attack birds scatter
like seed dropped from the feeder behind the station

both hawks always seem to leave satisfied
but by now you'd think the pigeons would catch on
yet every day birds line up
to take whatever spot is left
perhaps not knowing
that like other things in life and death
position won without struggle rarely brings safety
survival dependent not so much on chance
but on the willingness to fight for life

Wind

On our screened-in back porch
an overhead fan whap, whap, whaps
the heated scent of honeysuckle into the kitchen.
Sure, the windows are all open
but the only cool here is a frothy blue wave
painted on the side of a bowl of red hot chili peppers.

It's so hot inside, ice cubes disappear before you can pour
a glass full of tea or lemonade. It's so sun-bright outside,
sidewalk glare could blind someone walking west at dusk.
Two weeks ago, tar paper on the roof started dripping,
my grass turned brown, and the guy next door gave up
and sprayed his front yard green.

I simply ache for a wind to whip through the costal islands
lift the mainland flags and turn laughing gulls into
inland parking-lot birds for just one day.

I pray for the square white pennant with black center
to fly above the firestation so I can grab my sweater,
hit the streets & chant
a "cold-front, cold-front, cold-front" mantra.

You know, a week ago I said I'd trade
my hand-tooled leather matching purse and boots
for just one chilly day.
Today I simply wish for wings to fan the whole world cool.

ice cream bar

well, it's not exactly ice cream
although it is on a stick
frozen vanilla tofutti
dipped in deep dark chocolate
with organic sugar
no butter fat
no gluten added

bite into the crisp coating
a crunch then teeth slide
resistlessly into the rest
a double whammy of taste
if you can get used to it
not being ice cream

you stand atop wilting grass
beneath a blazing sun
watch dry clouds chase
across the sky like kids boats
scooting along a silken lake of blue

ice cream - tofutti - drips down
the stick onto your hand
the boats are yours
your breath the wind

Forming

not far from Galveston, I stand on a sandspit
in every direction but behind, water flows
a regular passage of time remarked
in waves, whitecaps, rivulets of brine
in a long-legged running of gulls behind the tide
its dark waters an exercise of thought, a meditation

discarding white ribbons of wake
a solemn procession of ships carve a channel from the bay
as bay becomes the land

a thousand suns float on bright ripples,
crystal facets topping the waves
and as the wind pushes clouds past lighthouse point
I become a solitary gull   a ship   a fish
a grain of sand upon the shore
a baby drifting in a cradle endlessly rocking
here on the timeless porch of America
at home next to the sea

island girl

the rip tide of the past
scours your beaches
with dark oceanic debris
cast away so long ago
It took a tsunami
of yesteryears
to thrust it onto shore
a storm of endless chaos
contradictions and avoidance
questions and denials
like a ship facing hurricane
you are trapped
by the very thing
that has kept you safe
you cannot flee
beyond the harbor
of the tiny island
of yourself

overhead, laughing gulls

across the seawall from east beach
two feet higher than the street
a pocket park lures a boy
the bright green postage stamp
lawn irresistible

he leaps up the slight rise
throws himself down into the shaggy grass
and rolls to rub away grains of sand
stuck to his wet swim suit and out between his toes.
he rolls and rolls coming to rest
in the slight shadow of his father's thin shade

you'll stain that white suit green, boy
the boy laughs and rolls some more
until the sun glides down the playground slide
to drop into the sandy gulf
tourists become street lamps
and the island and gulls dream

Pecan Season

A year ago, the night before your leave was up
we stood out behind the cabin, listened
to the cicada chorus near the creek bottom
the cries of geese migrating, breathed
in the acrid scent of wet leaves, laughed
at the damp fur smell of your ancient watchdog.
Then we scrubbed our nut-stained hands
with Lava soap under the pump and went inside.
I buried that old dog last week under his best blanket.
Today the telegram came. I read it out behind the cabin
before the north wind grabbed it up and out
across the yard and past the orchard where ground fog
still twists into the rolling hills. Tonight, if you listen close,
you can hear wet pecans fall from their husks
bounce through the branches
of the trees, roll down the tin roof.
They gathered gleaming on the ground
like the shining white stones resting
over all the girls and boys come home at last.

Witness

The spongy ground absorbs all morning sound
and a certain reverent hush surrounds
the volunteers who pace the Texas woods
of Arlington, Athens, Nacogdoches and beyond.

They examine each yard of ground
quiet concentration broken occasionally
by the placing of red flags and wrapping of yellow
police tape around squares of towering pines

bright markers for those who will follow later
dressed more carefully in contamination gear
and heavy gloves to carry away
broken particles of fallen craft.

Searchers share the point
aware that eyes must stay fresh to find
every piece of evidence, no matter how small
and so each in turn leads then follows.

But all keep private thoughts as still as the woods
for they have come not to grieve but to complete a mission
one begun weeks before by the crew of the Columbia
so long delayed in their return

the earthly findings merely symbolize
seven astronauts who glide
along some horizon we cannot view
forever sixteen minutes from home.

Congenital Defect

watching world news night after night
gawking numbly at road rage
gang wars, simple anger and strife
yet disputes amid nations
fights amongst factions
brawls between husband and wife
don't seem to matter on a private scale

what counts is the war we must wage
with the universe to decide if existence
is worthwhile in a world where hatred
rather than valve disorder may now be
the most common congenital defect
of the heart

at the edge of a dream

not all love is a brightness
that cloaks a far flung dreamer
it could be a bit of frayed memory
touching the stillness of a distant pool
perhaps a star's light that shines
out of a familiar patch of darkness
or a beacon reflected from night's pond

illuminating
first the black sky
then the tattered sleeping heart
calling the dreamer home

Waiting for the Late Night Train

Eyes focus on nothing in particular.
No one ever looks at your face,
hands juggle briefcases, evening
papers, hot coffee, cigarettes.
But he is difficult to ignore.
Standing behind the platform crowd
black hair long and tied back
face youthful, his ancient eyes
reveal nothing of what he knows
his feet patterning a rain dance.

Somehow, even here beneath the city's streets
in the rank and grimy subway tunnel,
treelands and woodsmoke cling to him...
so do your eyes.
His thoughts seem as well protected
as posts strung with razor wire
his heart a long red scarf
trapped in the wire's strands
setting it free could be risky
yet some primal instinct
demands you fall on bending knee
at his river's edge
but you turn away
fearful eyes searching
up and down the empty track
along the platform
anywhere but on him.
You, homebound, await the late night train
not mystery.

Anxious

She thinks her vision is dimming —
that the vivid blue jay and bright cardinal
the blinding color of the purple bunting
or the turning over of silver and blue waves
might fade at any moment into misty smoke.
She fears the quiet that darkness
should bring may instead be filled
with the alarming chittering of squirrels
or the surprising slither of pine needles
dropping through oak leaves to the ground
or the staccato chatter of sparrows
feeding from the plastic window feeder
or a disturbing rustle of a cowbird darting
under the bushes to eat sunflower seeds.
She dreads the footfalls of strangers
and worries that the unidentifiable will crowd in
until even the refuge of sleep could be denied
by startling creaking or unknown scraping
against the metal roof of the nursing home.
She resists laying down
and doses in the rocking chair
fearing that if she goes to bed
full darkness will descend
and no flashlight, candle or lamp
or even wishing
will ever illuminate her way again.

stop looking

who I am will not be discovered
from all of that which I am no more
do not look at things undone
or books bought but not yet read
scarves unraveled scavenged
for unused bits of yarn
I am not in any of those things
nor am I in the dozen dusty photos
set aside for fancy framing
or in sacks of gifts not yet given
look instead to the smile of my daughter
the laughter of my son
see me in the bright eyes of grandchildren
please present no invoice
against all the promises
I may still owe
accept what you find of me
in the music of my church
the generosity of my friends
the kindness of my husband
beneath these lines
        more done than awaiting
here I am

If Pandora comes

to gather back
her lost emotions
we'd all be better off
to hand back
anger, hate and fear.
But there was loss
and desperation
before that appalling box opened...
keep sorrow close
lest we forget
to mourn.

stainless steel sink

dirty hardy-plank town
brown as drought
no rain could green this grass

the train clacks slowly past
hometown girls and grease jockeys
laugh outside the corner store

if this were home, would I pour coffee
for the paunchy mailman who tips better
than the other 1:00 am drunks

would I wear pink and polish nails
or sweep the sidewalk
in front of the barbershop/hair salon

would I teach little Beths and Billies
how to push scales up and down
a battered tuneless piano

or would each day be like
used cups gathering in the bottom
of a scratched stainless sink

the wind drops pine needles as it pulls
the last of autumn from the trees —
the train jolts then moves faster — what's next?

Tethered in Llano Estacado

I rode westerly at dawn, and found
a mallard swimming listless circles in
a trailside cattle trough
his bright feathers jewel-like in the summer sun.
He made no move to fly:
a leather dipper tether tangled round his legs.
I put him on the ground and gently cut him loose.
He sat unmoving for the longest time,
until I finally threw him in the air.
The mallard lifted north toward Running Water Draw,
a hundred miles past the rocky hills and gulches
of my temporary home.
The bird had been as trapped
as I am now by circumstance and need
tethered tight by leather strands of memories.
I wonder – will I fly off alone
when life's sharp knife cuts me free?
Or will I wait for someone else
to toss me to the waiting sky?

Watching from Home

A black butterfly darts across the highway
headed for the median where city workers
plant a hundred or more flats of sweet alyssum
loose white petals tossed by the wind
reminiscent of the snowstorm
on the day of Kennedy's inauguration.

Outside, protected by the overhang
our hummingbird feeder, filled with sweet
red syrup, is covered in bees —
more than we've seen for years —
perhaps there will be honey in the spring.
At the corner of the yard, swan necks of Peace
rose canes thorn sharply down the side
of our storm damaged fence, racing to set roses
before their Valentine's day pruning.

One hundred million people watch television
a million cram into the DC mall
another million line the parade route
while here, over a thousand miles away
a hawk's cry turns inside out
the cloak of sparrows draped across
a fallen stand of Siberian sunflowers.

Each sighting and call seems etched upon this day
as tightly as the soft green gloves
warming our new First Lady's hands
while she smiles and holds the bible for her husband,
Barack Hussein Obama, newest American president
resolutely swearing in on the steps of history.

Winter Song

Snow has fallen
and so have I - fallen in love.
Thick clumps of snow flakes
drift toward and past me
like the streaming stars
of the Star Wars credits
long ago and far away
and everything has gone soft and quiet.
Window wipers freeze to windshields
ice covers windows and key holes
slicks the thin skating pond
of the walkway. I am so in love
with winter and the season
of urgent letter writing and quick replies
of navigating the slippery path
to stuff the mailbox with happy greetings
then slide back to the house again
upright and triumphant
holiday cards from friends
and family tucked beneath my chin
one hand clutching
a box of Aunt Harriet's
famous cream cheese cookies.
Snow has fallen
and so have I - fallen in love
with the joy of the season
and everything it represents
and once more
(for the thousandth time)
fallen in love again with you.

Silent, Soft and Slow

Frost like lace on frozen panes
glitters from each tattered weed.
Smoke spirals past the ice-glazed eaves
snowflakes spill like falling stars.

Snow lays its wreath upon the yard
shoes the feet of barren trees.
Ice slicks across the window sills
glints like silver buttons on new coats.

Fan-swirls mark where birds have flown
footprints map the track of tiny feet
when into autumn's empty rooms
tread winter's woe and joy.

reflections

crystal shadows pool
in lavender and lilac beneath the dogwoods
snowdrops drip
molting melting cellophane
brittle grasses break beneath our feet
robins lift from the path
snow geese trumpet
near the diamond-crusted fence
we inhale frozen winter
winter exhales liquid spring

Gardening

You're on your knees, hands deep in dirt
sweaty, stinky, tired, but close to the earth and to creation
yanking weeds, dead stalks and grass from the beds.
Where else would you start thinking about relationships
comparing store-bought pansies to tiny wild violets
both beautiful, but violets find their own way
into tame flower beds or scatter seed across the lawn
their progeny pushing broad grass blades aside.
This close to the earth and to creation
your mind fastens on bright yellow —
low marigolds, jasmine climbing up to the roof
trailing after sweet scent of roses and the smiles of friends.
You've been stung by sharp disappointment. Found thorny
raspberry vines, empty but for the bite that makes hands bleed
their sting as sharp as faithless friends
who smile to your face but mock at your back.
You on your knees at the start and the end of the day
try to pick out each thorn of disappointment and sorrow.
There is such hope in the garden
not just for a good harvest of food or beauty
a place for pulling out unwanted debris and unkindness
finding a few slivers of compassion exist, even for you.
If you dig in your soul deep enough
you might see a garden as a place to think more kindly
of those who have hurt you or you have hurt.
You may even find that we are all one.

floating beneath the surface tension

love persists in scraps and tatters
a small perfection in the jaggedness
of partly remembered dreams
when all wars ended with the last card turned

even when night seems emptiest
stars lean down to kiss each still pool of water
and if at last a moon appears
its brilliance riffles the edges of lakes

wind-ripples lap across oceans
make their slow way back again
there is no alone in nature, plants and planets
grow together and apart in harmony

beneath the surface of life
relationships quickly dispose
plastic bags, paper clothing, friendships
ripped apart at the seams

teach me how to fall

too often I fail or fall
out of support and appreciation
out of grace and understanding

teach me how to fall, if not with grace
then at least without breaking something
like breaking a promise or my heart or someone else's

self pity is a ravenous companion
withholding a chair to compassion
so teach me how to fall and fail well

I do it so very often, fail that is
show me ways to drop down lightly and scramble up again
perhaps with a smile, if not full, then at least genuine

I'd like to stop clutching the inevitable pain
teach me how to climb out of shadows
how to accept friendship offered and joy again

and if I must fail so very often
please teach me how to fall with grace

Branch of White Peonies and Pruning Shears
A painting by Edouard Manet

languidly sprawled
upon a sienna brown table
spreading petals
delicately curled at the edges
a branch of white blossoms
newly shorn
by a barely revealed
pair of pruning sheers

roses without thorns
like memories
of our mother's gardens
folded next to our hearts
not botanically precise
or completely accurate
but objects to invite study
of the relationships
between light and color
conveyed simply
fascinating
as a summer
operetta's
opening night
exquisitely described
yet uncomplicated
by informative detail

portrayed with
spontaneous brushwork
forms no more than suggested
all splendor revealed
as a receptacle of light
peonies rest
their crumpled shrouds
incarnate within
Manet's intent

Local Transport

You sleep amidst commotion
Logistics to one side
Transportation to the other
across the way the Mass Care desk.
You're not entitled to rest in a corner
your head on someone else's bulky satchel
their token of home a pillow beneath your head.
You don't travel from state to state
drive ERV's or staff shelter buses.
Your lot is to ferry folks
take them from their last Red Cross assignments
and start them out on something new.
Yet there you are asleep after trip five
you and the days sliding into one another
stacked like so many cases of water bottles
for the next crisis run at 6 am or 9:30, or 2
just waiting for someone to gently whisper
wake up now
another group needs their ride to the airport
come on now wake up.

Driving

They come from everywhere and go everywhere else:
South Dakota, Florida, Michigan, Illinois, Texas
Following Edouard, Fay
Gustav, Hanna, Ike
As Josephine fizzles, they watch for Kyle.
They rest on shelter cots, in sleeping bags on auditorium floors
Have done without ac, tv, and showers for weeks.
For them it's one Meal Ready to Eat after another
And barbeque, so much barbeque that the sight
Of one more plate smothered in red sauce
And the obligatory potato salad and coleslaw
Makes one man shake his head, sigh slow and say,
Thanks, but no.
They keep begging for the nearest sub shop or hoagie…
Does somebody know what day it is?
Anyone have a canister of mosquito repellent
Or an extra pair of clean dry socks?
Their faith is complete
Without a second thought
They hand over laundry and luggage to total strangers.
From the back of shuttles, cars, station wagons, vans
They call out encouragement to their couriers
Lost again from dodging downed power lines
Upended trees
Roadblocks in flooded neighborhoods.
They're looking for signs blown down by the wind
Trying to find the road, any road that leads towards chaos.
Call them tired at the end of extended tours,
Twenty-one days or more.
Call them new friends or temporary neighbors reassigned
Call them American Red Cross Volunteers.

we walk on rock and bone

wind pushing at our backs
it is not sorrow that makes us walk
nor is it fear
it is dumb stubbornness
and the refusal to die
where someone else wants
we walk the middle path
at first holding hands
then holding up the old the young
now carrying each other
leaning into the person ahead the person behind
refusing to leave any behind
we carry the living we carry the dead
wrapped in blankets of regret
but never covered with tears
we remember each face relive every moment
our children pick flowers at first
then pick at scabs and sores
wasted bodies stumble along
starve for food and freedom
covered in blankets of regret
but never wrapped in tears

no matter how hard the trail becomes
we bring determination with us
we leave behind our tears

so much time

spent peering through a looking glass
for your entry in the Book of the Dead
pouring over out-dated obituaries
for a description of your own life

you've forgotten the golden heat of sunflowers
the grace of maroon-tipped grasses bending with the wind
the sweetness of freshly laundered sheets
and plump pillows on your soft bed in this safe cool room

all you want is a hole someone else has dug for you
you're ticking tocks until a rattle-snaking exhalation
wishing for a goodbye of carpet grass pooling
around the bottom of a long mound of a rounded dirt pile

you try but fail to hide the shrouded envy
in your every staring look at the red notice
which blithely glows over your hospital room's door

every weakening muscle and screaming sinew
aching to take heed of that simple
sign's matter-of-fact advice
exit left

flute, bell, drum
>   for Rebecca Hatcher Travis

I play my mother's flute
and the sound it makes
becomes the wind

I lift my sister's bell
and the sound it makes
crumbles mountains

I beat my father's drum
and the sound it makes
echoes in my children

playing, ringing, drumming
passing on
the sounds of life

what is poetry

it is your voice
and not so much
what you say
but that you say it
melodic words
and sparkly thoughts
ideas persisting
like the endless
rush of blood moving
through the heart
your voice
keeping me engaged
alive with its presence

Award-winning American poet Mary Margaret Carlisle was born in Dallas, Texas. Published in numerous literary journals, magazines, and anthologies, Ms. Carlisle is a member of The Texas Association of Creative Writing Teachers, four chapters of the Poetry Society of Texas, the Bay Area Writers League, Galveston Poets Roundtable, Women Who Write, and the Academy of American Poets, among others. Magna Cum Laude graduate of University of Houston – Clear Lake, she was honored with keys from Phi Kappa Phi and Alpha Chi in 1991. In 1988, she was inducted into PEN, the National Writing Society. She's been a featured poet across Texas, including for the Poetry Society of Texas, Poets Unleashed, First Friday, Poetry in the Arts, Bay Area Barnes & Noble, and others. She is a Councilor for the Poetry Society of Texas, and is the founder and President of the Gulf Coast Poets. She created the Coffee Oasis Reading Series. In 2008, Poets & Writers, Inc. bestowed her with a grant to present a scholarly lecture about the 2008 United States' Poets Laureates. She has taught over 75 workshops and facilitates Poetry Works Workshops in the Texas Bay Area. Director of Sol Magazine Projects, she chairs the *Ampersand Poetry Journal* board. Her father was a published poet, as is her younger sister. Ms Carlisle lives in Webster, Texas, with her photographer/web designer husband Leo F. Waltz. They volunteer for the American Red Cross.

Poems in this book appeared in:

mockingbird riff - *2008 Texas Poetry Calendar*, editors Scott Wiggerman and David Meischen, Dos Gatos Press.

tincan summer - *The Houston Poetry Fest 2004 Anthology*, editor Robert Clark.

Father and the Furnace - *Windows 2004*, editor Gilbert Benton, Alvin Community College.

dipping crawdads - *The Weight of Addition: an anthology of Texas Poetry*, editor Randall Watson, Mutabilis Press.

Perennial - *Houston International Poetry 3 for Peace Anthology*, co-editors Lisa Grable and Glynn Monroe Irby.

In my Native Tongue – *TimeSlice: Houston Poetry 2005*, editor Carolyn Tourney Florek, Mutabilis Press

River Road Mantras – *2010 Texas Poetry Calendar*, editor Scott Wiggerman, Dos Gatos Press.

Lost Peak Touches Heaven - *Mountain Time: A Poetry Anthology*, editor Tom Davis, Old Mountain Press.

Gadwall Duck Pond, West Texas - 1) *2006 Texas Poetry Calendar*, editors Scott Wiggerman and David Meischen, Dos Gatos Press; 2) *Big Land, Big Sky, Big Hair: Best of the Texas Poetry Calendar*, editor Scott Wiggerman, Dos Gatos Press.

With the Moon for a Lantern - *Night Whispers: A Poetry & Prose Anthology*, editor by Tom Davis, Old Mountain Press.

island girl - *Sand, Sea, & Sail: A Poetry and Prose Anthology*, editor Tom Davis, Old Mountain Press.

Pecan Season - *2009 Texas Poetry Calendar*, editors Scott Wiggerman and Cindy Huyser, Dos Gatos Press.

Witness - *Lean Seed 2003*, editor Michael Woodson, San Jacinto College Press.

Tethered in Llano Estacado - *Texas Poetry Calendar 2000*, editors Lianne Mercer and Betty Davis, Flying Cow Productions.

Congenital Defect - *Windows 2002*, editor, Gilbert Benton, Alvin Community College.